# HOW TO SURVIVE WHEN (YOU THINK) THERE'S NOTHING TO DO

by Suzanne Francis

HOW TO SURVIVE ANYTHING CLUB

SCHOLASTIC INC.

New York Toronto London Auckland Sydney
Mexico City New Delhi Hong Kong Buenos Aires

No part of this publication may be reproduced in whole or in part, or stored in a retrieval system, or transmitted in any form or by any means, electronic, mechanical, photocopying, recording, or otherwise, without the written permission of the publisher. For information regarding permission, please write to Scholastic Inc., Attention: Permissions Department, 557 Broadway, New York, NY 10012.

ISBN: 0-439-57906-6

Design: Julie Mullarkey Gnoy
Illustrations: Kelly Kennedy

Copyright © 2004 by Scholastic Inc.

All rights reserved. Published by Scholastic Inc.

SCHOLASTIC, HOW TO SURVIVE ANYTHING, and associated logos are trademarks and/or registered trademarks of Scholastic Inc.

12 11 10 9 8 7 6 5 4 3 2         5 6 7 8 9/0

Printed in the U.S.A.

First Scholastic printing, July 2004

# CONTENTS

**How to Survive This Book** ............................................. 4

**You've Got Game(s)—Boggle and Checkers** ..................... 6
...the basic rules and a few versions of these classic games with a twist!

**Lights Out!—Games to Play in the Dark** ....................... 14
...including Night Assassin, Flashlight Tag, and The Remains of Mr. X

**On Your Mark, Get Set—Games to Play Outdoors** ......... 26
...including Sock Jug, Toilet Paper Toss, and Wiffle Bat Beach Ball Hockey

**On the Move—Games to Play on the Go** ...................... 31
...including Frifflezooter, Red Car, Black Car, and Monkey

**All Hands on Deck—Card Games** ................................ 46
...including I Doubt It!, My Ship Sails, and Snap!

**Magic Tricks—Now You See It, Now You Don't** .............. 52
...including Magic Cup-O-Water, Mummy Finger, and Pet Elephant

**Use Your Head—Games to Tease Your Brain** .................. 65
...including Super Sleuth, Invention Grab Bag, and Backtalk

**Boredom Busters Forever!** ........................................... 80

# How to Survive This Book

**O**kay, so the chances that you'll get shipwrecked on a deserted island or stranded on a mountaintop without food or water are pretty slim, but there is one sitch that causes fun-loving kids everywhere to get the jitters—having NOTHING to do! And, on the days that you're cooped up inside because it's raining, or you're stuck in the car (with your annoying little sib, who won't leave you alone), or you're just hanging out, sometimes you can't help but wonder how you're going to SURVIVE. *"I'm soooooo BORED!"* you say. *"There's NOTHING to do!"*

Well, go ahead and say those words loud and proud because if you're holding this book in your hands, it'll be the *last* time you'll say them! Go ahead, say them again if you want to, but *that* will be the absolute *last* time you'll say them because you're getting closer to all the fun that's revealed in this book—and once you've discovered all these things to do, *I'm soooooo BORED!* and *There's NOTHING to do!* won't be a part of your vocabulary anymore!

**How to Survive When (You Think) There's Nothing to Do will give you the stuff you need to boot Boredom right out the door!** Whether Boredom's waiting for you when you get home from school, at a friend's house, or even on your next family vacation (Boredom just *loves* long car trips!), you'll be ready!

To get you started, "You've Got Game(s)" shows you how to play the two mini games you received with this book: **Boggle** and **Checkers**, as well as fun variations on the original rules.

The games come on a handy dandy keychain so you can carry them around and play whenever you want, wherever you are.

"Lights Out!" has lots of ghoulishly fun and spooky stuff to try in the dark. **Want to catch some ghosts? Like telling super-scary stories?** Then this section's for you!

"On Your Mark, Get Set" features a bunch of games to play outdoors with one friend (and sometimes a bunch more).

If it's time for the family road trip again, or just another "quick" trip to the store with mom, "On the Move" is the section for you! With games like **License Plate Word Storm** and **Eagle Eye**, you'll wonder how you got there (and back) so quickly!

**There are plenty of card games to play** in "All Hands on Deck," which are sure-fire Boredom busters.

And what's a book of fun without a few tricks up its sleeves? *Magic tricks*, that is! In "Magic Tricks—Now You See It, Now You Don't," **you'll learn how to magically restore a ripped-up photo, stick a pin in a balloon without popping it, and make your very own live mummy finger**! (And by then, you'll find that you've made Boredom *disappear,* too!)

Who says you have to have a lot of stuff on hand to have a good time? Blast Boredom away with brain power! "Use Your Head" is full of **mind games, word games, and creative ways to tease your brain**.

So get ready to look Boredom square in the eye and shout *"You know what, Boredom? I'm bored of YOU!"*

# You've Got Game(s)— Boggle and Checkers

It's always great to have friends over, but when it's time to figure out what you want to do together, it sometimes goes like this: *"What do you want to do?" "I don't know. What do you want to do?" "I don't know. What do you want to do?"* This can go on for what feels like forever, until finally, someone blurts out *"There's never anything to do around here!"* Well, guess what? There are always *lots* of things to do around here, there, and everywhere!

First up: your new and nifty mini games, **Boggle** and **Checkers**. Yes, we know instructions came with your games, *but* if you want to know here and now **how to play** (or if you lost those little pieces of paper already!), here they are. But wait—there's more! There are also **tips, tricks, and strategies** on how to play your best, and you'll also find different versions of these games to play and get some ideas for **other fun things you can do** with your new gadgets!

## BOGGLE

**What You'll Need:** Your Boggle mini game, paper, pencils (one for each player)

**Players:** 2 or more

Put your thinking cap on nice and snug because Boggle is a game for your brain! To play, give each player a piece of paper and a pencil. Slide out the timer in your Boggle set (yes, it's supposed to come apart!) and put it aside. Now take the cube and shake up the letters inside. Make sure you mix 'em up really well! Give your wrist a real workout! Once you're sure they're good and mixed (or maybe when your hand starts to feel like it'll fall off—*just kidding*), get the letter cubes to settle down into the grid so that they all lay flat.

## Survival Tip

If your cubes aren't settling right, tap one side of the box with the heel of your hand. If that doesn't work, try asking the letters nicely, or just keep on tapping till they obey you and lie flat!

Everyone set and settled? Good. **Now the object of the game is for all the players to find as many words as they can, from one shake of the letters, in three minutes** (that's where the timer comes in—more on that in a moment). The letters have to be connected *and* in order—but they can be joined horizontally, vertically, or diagonally, to the left, right, or up and down. No letter cube can be used more than once within a single word (but of course, you can use the same letter twice, as long as it's on two cubes). All the players have three minutes to write down as many words as they can find. (The timer attached to your Boggle set is one minute long, so you'll have to flip it an extra two times to get your full three minutes.)

Once your time is up, each player reads off his list of words. Any word that appears on more than one player's list, gets crossed off everybody's lists. After everyone has read their lists, each player adds up their score (points listed below) for any remaining words.

For example, if you had the words "moose," "help," and "freedom," you'd get 2 points for "moose," 1 point for "help," and 5 points for "freedom"—a whopping total of 8 points!

| | |
|---|---|
| **3–4 letter words** | = 1 point each |
| **5 letter words** | = 2 points each |
| **6 letter words** | = 3 points each |
| **7 letter words** | = 5 points each |
| **8 letters or more** | =11 points each |

## Survival Tip

Don't forget to scan all the words you find—there could be another sneaky word hiding in there! For example, if you've found the word "bear," look closer and you'll find the word "ear". Pretty slick, huh?

**ANOTHER TIP:** It always helps to look at a problem from another angle. If you feel like you can't find any more words, turn the cube around to get a new view. Just think: there are four different sides to the cube, so there are four different angles to look at the letters from. Switch it up and you may be surprised at how many words you see that you didn't see before!

**TRAINING TIP:** Speed is important in this game. If you want to be in training for the pros, you've got to practice! Set the timer and see if you can beat your own high score. How many words can you find in a minute? Race yourself!

## SWADNUL

**What You'll Need:** Your Boggle mini game, paper, pencil
**Players:** 1 or more

No, *swadnul* isn't a real word. Boggle helped invent it to mean…this game! Haven't you ever wished you could talk in code to your friends? **Use your Boggle mini game to invent your own secret language!** Come up with some words or a sentence that you and your friends can secretively say. Shake up the letters and write them down in order, from left to right, top to bottom. Now break down the letters to invent words. Assign meanings to the words, and write them down so you remember. You can even make up your own secret dictionary!

## SUPER 16

**What You'll Need:** Your Boggle mini game, paper, pencils
**Players:** 1 or more

If you like good old-fashioned word searches and love finding words, **write down all the letters your shake of the Boggle cube gives you—and go wild**. You don't have to make sure the letters are connected to make a word—you can use the letters in any order you want, just as long as they turn up in the grid! Give yourself a time limit. If playing with a friend, see who comes up with the most words. Who comes up with the most unique ones? The longest? With 16 letters, there are lots of possibilities!

## CHECKERS

Feel like jumping, capturing, and being crowned? Or do you want to know what all that means first? Well, read on and get ready to challenge a friend to a battle of the minds!

**What You'll Need:** Your Checkers mini game
**Players:** 2

**Keep those thinking caps on because there's no time for zoning out while playing Checkers.** You have to think on your feet! (Not literally, of course. You should definitely be sitting—these games can take awhile!) But before you do anything, release the clasp on the side of your Checkers set and unfold your very cool and pocket-friendly board. (Don't you just love the way you can carry it around in your pocket?) Now slide out the handy dandy side drawer and remove twelve checkers of each color (your set comes with sixteen of each, in case you lose some). Sit on one side of the board and set up the checkers on the twelve black squares that are closest to you. Look at the picture to see what we mean. Your friend should do the same on the opposite side of the board with his color checkers on the twelve black squares closest to him.

All set up? Good. Black should move first. (We're not sure why—it's a Checkers thing.) Move your checker one square diagonally (left or right) towards your opponent's side of the board. Remember: Checkers is played only on the black squares, so if you find yourself on a red square—oops! Get back on black! **Okay, so you're going to move your checkers diagonally across the board, one square at a time, towards the opposite side of the board, taking turns with your opponent, of course.** The object of the game is to be the last player able to make a move. Ready? Wait, you're not ready yet! First, let's go over jumping (or capturing) and crowning: moves and rules for playing the game.

**JUMPING** (also called *capturing*)**:** How do you jump over a checker? No, you don't need a pogo stick or a good pair of sneakers for this kind of jumping! Your opponent's checker has to be positioned diagonally in front of yours, and there has to be an empty space diagonally *behind* his checker for you to land on. Basically, you're leaping over his checker and landing on the space right behind him. Think of it as if you were jumping over a stone, *while staying on a path*. **If you jump one of your opponent's checkers, you get to keep it.** (That's why jumping is also called capturing.)

## Survival Tip

If you're double- or triple-jumping, you can jump diagonally left *and* right. Use this to your advantage! If you jump diagonally to the left for the first leap, you can go diagonally *right* for the second leap (as long as there's room for you to land). Look for these extra ways to take your opponent by surprise and capture several of his checkers in one swoop! Zig-zag your way across the board, if you can, and watch your opponent's jaw drop!

**DOUBLE- OR TRIPLE- JUMPING:** Shock and amaze your opponent by leaping over two or three of his checkers at once! It works just like the single jump, but after you land, if there's *another* one of your opponent's checkers diagonally in front of you again, then you can jump it in the same move, too—as long as there's a space diagonally behind the last checker you jump to land on. Remember, you can't land on red squares!

### CHEATER ALERT!

If you see the opportunity to jump, you *have* to do it—yes, even if it puts your checker in a position to be captured.

**CROWNING:** If one of your checkers makes it all the way across to the edge of your opponent's side of the board, it will be *crowned* a King. Imagine that? Instant royalty! Sorry, this doesn't mean you can snap your fingers and someone will instantly bring you cookies, but it *does* mean you get to place an extra same-colored checker on top of the checker that made it to your opponent's edge of the board. Every one of your checkers that gets to the opposite end of the board gets crowned in the same way. **This double-decker checker is a King.** And a King is special because it not only moves diagonally forward across the board, like the other checkers can, but *diagonally backwards,* too. Your King can be a big help in capturing because of its ability to move both ways. Watch out, though—Kings (if they move back across the board into play) can get captured, too!

When a player has no pieces left, or is completely blocked and can't make a move, he loses, *so think before you move*!

Makes sense? Then get going! And like anything else, keep on playing and your game will improve faster than a speeding zig-zag triple jump!

### Survival Tip

In Checkers, it can help to try and predict where your opponent will go *before* you make your move, so *you* can move wisely.

## CHUMP CHECKERS

**What You'll Need:** Your Checkers mini game
**Players:** 2

Losing is winning when you play Chump Checkers! It's played just like regular Checkers—except it's the complete *opposite*: the first player to lose all of his pieces wins! The object of the game is to try and place your pieces where your opponent can capture (jump) them. **TWO RULES:** first, you *have* to capture your opponent's pieces if they're in position to be jumped. (And no pretending you don't see it! Open those eyes!) Second, there's no crowning in this game. **If you make it to the opposite end of the board, you just turn around and come back—like a true chump!**

## ROYAL CHECKERS

**What You'll Need:** Your Checkers mini game
**Players:** 2

There may be no crowning in Chump Checkers, but in Royal Checkers, everyone's a King! To set up this game, each player chooses a color and sits at *opposite corners* of the board. Set up six checkers in your corner—you and your opponent's checkers should all be set up on the same colored squares (either all black, like in regular Checkers, or all red, for this variation). You should have two checkers in the two squares closest to you in your corner, and four checkers in the four squares in front of those (look at the picture to see what we mean).

All ready? The checkers are still moved diagonally, but **since every checker in Royal Checkers is a King (they just aren't crowned), they can move forward and backwards diagonally**. Also, in this game, you can jump over your own checker if it's in front of you. (This doesn't count as a capture, since it's your own guy.) The object of the game is to be the first to capture all your opponent's pieces and be crowned the Royal Winner!

## Silly Uses for Your Checkers and Boggle!

1. Hang mini reminder notes on the fridge with one of your magnetic checkers.

2. Use them as dog (or cat) tags.

3. Form a band! They make great maracas (give them a shake and see, but be sure your checkers are in their drawer, not on the playing board, when you do!).

4. Use them as cowbells (if you happen to have any cows!).

5. Hang them up as wind chimes.

6. Put them in your **Car Survival Kit** (see page 41 for details).

7. Clip them to your shoelaces to put a little rattle in your step.

8. Use them to hypnotize your goldfish (if you've got one!).

What else? How many other silly uses can you think of for your Checkers and Boggle?

# Lights Out!—Games to Play in the Dark

**W**ant to know a sure-fire way to kiss Boredom goodnight? Hit the lights! No, we don't mean go to sleep! Turn off the lights and get ready to play some great games in the dark!

Some of the things to do in this section are scary, and some are even scarier. But, all of them are guaranteed to thrill you and chill you!

**REMEMBER: JUST BECAUSE IT'S DAY TIME DOESN'T MEAN YOU CAN'T PLAY IN THE DARK!**

Or perhaps it's night time in the summer, but still light out. Either way, if it's too bright out, you can create your own night-time space.

Try these tactics for instant midnight:

*DOES ANYONE REMEMBER WHERE THE LIGHT SWITCH IS?*

- **Play in a walk-in closet or another small space** where you can block out all the light (it's best if your game doesn't involve a lot of running around). *Scary!*

- **Make a tent.** Throw some blankets or sheets over some chairs and climb under. *Spooky!*

- **Wear a blindfold.** Use a bandanna or a scarf (or any length of cloth that you can tie around your head). *Creepy!*

## NIGHT ASSASSIN

See if you can spot the Assassin before he spots you—if you don't, you're dead meat!

**What You'll Need:** Flashlights (one for every player), paper, scissors, pencil
**Players:** 4 or more

In this game, nobody's safe! The detectives (who are all the players other than the one Assassin) try to figure out who the Assassin is, while the Assassin tries to get them! How does the Assassin get someone? In the blink of an eye! All the Assassin has to do is make eye contact and wink at you, and you're a goner.

First, cut up squares of paper to make cards—cut as many squares as you have players. Mark one of the cards with an X and leave the rest blank. Fold up each square and shuffle them so that no one knows where the X is. Each player chooses one of the slips of paper and secretly looks at it. **The person who gets the X is the "Assassin"** and the players who get blank slips are the "Detectives". But no one knows for sure who's who. Everyone's a suspect, so put on your best poker face! ("Poker face" is a term used to describe what you look like when you show no expression at all. That way, no one knows what you're thinking—or who you really are!)

**Now it's time to hit the lights, grab your flashlights, and sit in a circle.** Each player holds a flashlight up under his chin so it's shining up on his face. This way, everyone can see everyone else's eyes in the dark. To play the game fairly, make sure you look around the circle from person to person—*at their eyes*. Don't pretend to look at the floor or at a bump in the ceiling just so the Assassin can't wink at you! That's no fun—or fair!

If the Assassin *does* make eye contact and wink at you, you have to say, *"I've been hit!"* Then, turn off your flashlight and lie on the floor. If you're into drama and you like to play it up, you can take the opportunity to perform an elaborate and dramatic death scene! **Feel free to scream, groan, stick your tongue out, and flop around on the floor like a fish!** You might as well entertain everyone before you're out for the count!

During the game, all the detective players scan the circle to try and catch the Assassin in the act of winking—at someone else. (Remember: if the Assassin winks at you, it's too late! You're dead, and you can't reveal who he is!) If at any time a detective player thinks he knows who the Assassin is, he can say *"I suspect"* and says the name of the player he thinks is the Assassin. If he guesses right, he wins the game. If he guesses wrong, he's out of the game and dead himself. Keep playing until the Assassin gets everyone out, or until a detective player guesses who the Assassin is. Then shuffle up and distribute new slips of paper (one marked with an X), deal them out, and play again!

## PASS THE FLASHLIGHT

In this game, you and your friends try to scare the pants off each other while twisting your own horrid tale any which way you like! And yes, of course…it's played in the dark!

**What You'll Need:** A flashlight
**Players:** 2 or more

Sit in a circle with your friends—*in the dark*! The person who will start off this very wicked tale should have the flashlight. How does the story start? Are you in a dark, dank, desolate, ghost-infested house? Or maybe the story begins in the cobwebby and dusty coffin of a vampire about to awaken? It's totally up to the first player. The only rule is to try and make it as scary as possible!

**After the first player starts off the story with a few lines, she should pass the flashlight to the next person, who continues the dark tale.** You never know where the story's going because it's always up to the next player. This way, everyone is surprised! Leave everyone hanging at an exciting moment in your story right before you pass the flashlight, so your neighbor has to think fast! For example, if you began

your story with *"One late, late, night, there was a girl who rode her bike through the cemetery…"* you could, before passing the flashlight, add *"The girl felt something brush by her cheek. When she looked down, there was a cold, stone tomb and she saw a…."* If you stopped there and passed the flashlight to the next player, he'd have to think fast and tell us what the girl saw in the tomb! Continue playing until someone thinks the story should end—or you scare yourselves too much and want to stop!

## Survival Tip

Details can be scary! Don't speed ahead! Slow it down! Take the time to describe what's happening in your story. Send chills down everyone's spine by setting the scene. For example, if you started telling a story about a haunted house, you could say *"There was a haunted house…"* and then go right on to the rest of your story. But if you really wanted to paint a picture and get people sitting on the edge of their seats, you could say something like *"In the woods, behind a forest of gnarled black trees, there is a house made completely of bones."* Ahhh! *That* story sounds a lot creepier!

**ONE MORE TIP:** Use that flashlight! Put it up under your chin and have it shine on your face for a creepy look while you spin your tale. Or use it to shine on the ceiling, if there's a full moon in your story. If you're talking about a fierce thunder and lightning storm, you could flash the flashlight on and off. Try and think of different things you can do with your flashlight to make your story even scarier!

**THIS REALLY IS THE LAST TIP:** Use sound effects to spice up your story! You might, say, knock on the floor to signal a knock at the door. Or use your voice to form moans, groans, growls, shrieks, and screams to surprise and shock the other players and make everyone's hair stand on end!

## Some Scary Topics for Your Stories

- Graveyards
- Haunted houses
- Mummies
- Storms
- Werewolves
- Spider webs
- Giant spiders and insects
- Things that float or levitate
- Vampires
- Coffins
- Witches
- Deserted places
- A burial ground
- The full moon
- Monsters
- Trap or secret doors
- Bats

Get the idea? Think of others, if you'd like, before you start storytelling—for maximum creepy effect!

## FLASHLIGHT TAG

It's scarier (and more fun!) to hide in the dark! Play Flashlight Tag to get your heart pumping and your teeth chattering!

**What You'll Need:** A flashlight
**Players:** 4 or more

In this game, the person who is "It" is the only one with a flashlight. Everyone else is in the dark! (The flashlight should stay on at all times and shouldn't be covered—it's tougher for "It" to sneak up on people that way!)

To start the game, the player who's "It" should close her eyes and count to 100 while everyone else hides. After counting, the person who's "It," with the help of her trusty flashlight, searches for everyone. **When she spots someone, she should shine her flashlight on the player to "tag" them.** Once a player is tagged, he joins "It" and has to help find the others. This continues until only one player is left hidden. The last player standing becomes the new "It".

Hiders are always free to move from their hiding places, so if you see "It" coming your way, and can get away and hide somewhere else before she spots you, do it, if you dare!

## Ghost Flashlight Tag!

**What You'll Need:** Soda cans (two for each player), pebbles, duct tape, flashlight

**Players:** 4 or more

Clean out some empty soda cans and put some noisy pebbles in them. Tape the opening holes shut, and what do you have? Instant ghost rattlers! Tape a ghost rattler to everyone's ankles, or to the tops of their feet. Now play Flashlight Tag again, but—this time—good luck trying to walk softly and stay hidden!

# FLASHLIGHT SARDINES

Warning: playing this game might make you feel like a sardine!

**What You'll Need:** Flashlights (one for each player)
**Players:** 3 or more

One person gets picked to be the "Hider" and hides, while all the seekers (everybody else) stay together and close their eyes and count out loud to 100. Once they get to 100, the seekers separate and start searching for the Hider. Once a seeker finds the Hider, he should fight the urge to yell *"I found her! I found her! Hey, guys! I found her!"* Instead, he should *quietly* turn off his flashlight and join her in her hiding spot. Squeeze in there, you sardine! You don't want anyone to find you! This continues until the last seeker finds everyone and joins the by-now-really-crowded hiding place!

*WHAT'S TAKING CHRIS SO LONG?*

## Survival Tip

When you're the Hider, remember that everyone has to fit in the space you hide in (if they find you, that is)! So, think twice before wedging yourself into the cabinet—it could get awfully squishy in there!

## GHOSTS IN THE GRAVEYARD

Get ready to run like a ghost in this game!

**What You'll Need:** Just you and your fast feet
**Players:** 3 or more

**This game should be played outside (in the dark, of course!)** so you have lots of space to run! First, pick a tree or a place to be home base. This is the only safe place to be when the Ghost comes out—you can't get tagged when you're on home base. Everywhere else is considered the "graveyard". *Ooooooooh!*

Choose one person to be the "Ghost". Everyone else is on the "Graveyard Patrol Team" ("GPT" for short) and their job is to check the graveyard for ghosts. To start the game, those on the GPT go to home base, close their eyes, and count, as the Ghost hides. No peeking! (That would totally violate GPT code!) The players should slowly count out loud: *"One o'clock, no ghost, two o'clock, no ghost, three o'clock, no ghost…"* all the way up to *"midnight, yes ghost!"* When they reach *"midnight,"* they all (no stragglers!) have to leave the base and search the graveyard for the Ghost.

The first patroller to spot the Ghost yells, *"Ghost in the graveyard!"* and everyone tries to run back to home base before getting tagged by the Ghost. The Ghost tries to capture as many patrollers as he can. Whoever he manages to tag will join him in the ghostly graveyard world and become a ghost, too. When everybody on the GPT goes back to home base (or gets tagged), they should start counting again while the ghosts hide, but the GPT better watch out! The ghosts in the graveyard have multiplied and you never know who's going to be tagged next!

**Keep playing until there is only one player left untagged in the graveyard**—then start over again. The winner gets to be the new Ghost!

## 10 Scary or Silly Things to Say in the Dark

1. It smells like werewolf in here.
2. Boo! (Okay, that was an easy one, unless it was unexpected enough to scare you!)
3. Uh-oh. I think my brother's pet spider got out!
4. Shh! Did anyone else hear that scratching on the window?
5. I just felt a ghost!
6. There's something coming through the floor!
7. The fireplace is whispering to me!
8. I see dead people!
9. Please tell me those are *your* hairy hands on my hand.
10. Whose foot is this? It's not attached to a body!

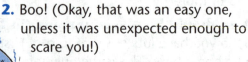

## THE REMAINS OF MR. X

You can probably tell by this game's title that it's not going to be pretty. But if the thought of gross, disgusting, horrific, creepy, and nasty things delights you, then you *don't* want to miss this game! (Just don't plan on playing right after a meal, or you just might lose your lunch!)

**What You'll Need:** Some or all of these (or your other variations on the theme): a rubber glove, cold cooked spaghetti, corn silk, a hot dog, a lemon, un-popped popcorn, grapes, cornflakes, dried apricots, jelly, uncooked noodles, a big marshmallow, a carrot, various-sized boxes or paper bags, tape, blindfolds, paper, pencils

**Players:** 2 or more

**This game is all about being grossed out and grossing out your friends!** Anything that's this creepy takes some prep, so you'll need a little time to get everything ready. First, get all Mr. X's "body parts" together and put each part into its own box or paper bag. If you're using boxes, cut a hole in the box top, just big enough for your friends to fit their hands in. Then after you put the nastiness in the box, tape the top on (with the hole). This way, the other players won't be able to see what they're feeling. Or, if you're using bags, just have the other players wear blindfolds when they're feeling the stuff (or, at least, close their eyes, if they promise not to peek). Remember to mark each box or bag with its correct "body part" so you know what's what!

Here's what you'll need (or need to do) and what each item is meant to be:

- **Fill a rubber glove with water,** tie it off, and freeze it for Mr. X's **hand**.

- Put some **peeled grapes in the freezer**—these are Mr. X's **eyeballs**.

- An ear of corn doesn't feel like anyone's ear we know, but **take some of its corn silk** (that hairy stuff at the top) off and you've got some of Mr. X's **hair**.

- **Use dried apricots** for Mr. X's **elbow skin**. (Gross!)

- **Break off the big end of a carrot** for Mr. X's **big toe**.

- **Grab some un-popped kernels of corn** for Mr. X's **teeth**.

- **A cold piece of a hot dog** can be the tip of Mr. X's **nose**—yuck!

- **Slice a lemon wedge** and squeeze the juice out. What's left can be Mr. X's **lips**.

- **Cold cooked spaghetti** feels just like Mr. X's **brains**.

- Mr. X's **fingernails** are just like **raw noodles**. Break some off and put them in a box.
- **Pour some jelly** into a little baggie and pop it into the box or bigger bag. This is Mr. X's **heart**.
- **Squash a big marshmallow** for Mr. X's **tongue**.
- **Crush some cornflakes** for Mr. X's **scabs**—ew!

## Survival Tip

Find and feel some stuff around your kitchen (in the fridge, especially) and elsewhere in your house to see what other nasty things you can use! Close your eyes to test it out.

Okay, now that you've put together all of Mr. X's remains, you're ready to get creative. It's up to you to write a story about Mr. X, and yes—it should be scary and gross and creepy and all the rest!

**Use the body parts in the story, so that when you read or tell the story to your friends, you can have them feel what you're reading or telling about.** It'll definitely gross them out! For example, in telling the story of Mr. X, you could say something like *"Mr. X had a dandruff problem and this caused a lot of scabs to form on his head because he'd scratch like a maniac. Feel this box full of his scabs!"* Then you'd put your friend's hand in that box of crushed cornflakes and he'd probably feel like he might toss his cookies (that's why it's not a good idea to play this game right after lunch or supper, especially if you're squeamish)! Ick! You could continue your story by saying *"Mr. X was so busy scratching (as usual) one day that he wasn't paying attention to where he was going. That's how he stubbed his big left toe right on top of a vampire's tomb stone. We still have the left big toe that Mr. X stubbed. Here it is. Hold his toe while I tell you what happened next."* Then you'd give the player a box with the carrot piece to feel. Get it? Pretty great and gross, huh?

If you want to see if your friends can guess what you used to make the body parts, pass out paper and pencils, and while you're reading or telling your story, let them each write down what they think they're touching. Or maybe you don't want them to guess because there's nothing *to* guess— maybe you insist that each one really *is* a body part that belongs to the remains of Mr. X!

## PITCH DARK ART

**What You'll Need:** Paper, pencils (one for each player)
**Players:** 2 or more

Give everyone some paper and a pencil. It should be totally dark for this game—if it's not, the artists can wear blindfolds. **Choose one person to be the storyteller, and all the other players are the artists.** The storyteller will think of a scene to slowly describe to the artists, while they draw it out. For example, she could say first *"There once was a very old house high up on a hill."* Then she'd give everyone time to draw the image, and then continue on with something like *"On this one particular night, there was a terrible storm."* Once they finished drawing that step, she'd go on again. *"That was the night that a vampire knocked on the front door."* The storyteller should continue to give the artists direction until each picture is done, but keep in mind that you don't want to give too many steps. Once the artists have finished their pictures, take off their blindfolds or turn on the lights to check out the results! It's not easy drawing in the dark!

# On Your Mark, Get Set—Games to Play Outdoors

**F**ace it, just because people call it the "great outdoors" doesn't mean you'll always have a great time—unless you have this book handy! Between **flying toilet paper relays** to a great game of **wiffle bat beach ball hockey**, you'll find out how you and some friends can have a fun-tastic time!

## WACKY RACES

If you have enough friends over to make up two teams, you're all set to race. We're not talking about a good old-fashioned running race—although, give it a go if you're up for it. We're talking about kooky, weird, wild, and WACKY RACES. The kind that can make you laugh until your cheeks hurt and your side splits! Read on to get in on the fun!

### FEARLESS FLYING TOILET PAPER

**What You'll Need:** Squares of toilet paper, drinking straws (one for each player)
**Players:** 6 or more

In this race, blow through a straw to keep a small square of toilet paper afloat as you race to the finish line. Don't let that flying T.P. fall! If it does, you've got to start from the beginning! First team to have all their players fly their toilet paper to the finish line wins.

### WIFFLE SPOON

**What You'll Need:** Two wiffle balls, spoons (one for each player)
**Players:** 6 or more

Each team member carries the wiffle ball across the finish line…with a spoon in his mouth! Divide up into two teams and pick a point for everybody to race to, like a tree or a fence. No hands, feet, or anything but the spoon on that wiffle ball, please! If you drop it, scoop it back up (without your hands)! First team to have all their members run to that point and back with the wiffle ball is the winner!

## THE BALLOON BETWEEN US

**What You'll Need:** Inflated balloons
**Players:** 8 or more

Grab a partner because you can't do this one alone! Stand back to back, and place an inflated balloon in between you and your partner. Here comes the hard part: work together to make it to the finish line while keeping the balloon between you. Did you drop it? It's okay—try again! First pair to get to the finish line is the winner.

**VARIATION:** Try using a water balloon for some super-soaking summer fun!

## GET DRESSED!

**What You'll Need:** Lots of different kinds of hats, like ski hats, baseball caps, shower caps, top hats—the wackier they are, the more laughs you'll get!

**Players:** 6 or more

Ever wished you were a little bit taller? Here's your chance! Divide into two teams. The first player for each team puts on an assigned number of hats (the sillier the better!), then runs to the end of the course and comes back to the start, trying not to drop any hats (if she does, she'll have to start over!). The next player puts on the hats, does the same, and so on, until the whole team has done it. First team to have all of their players finish wins. Try not to laugh too hard at your teammates—you're next!

# BIG FOOT

**What You'll Need:** Four of the biggest shoeboxes you can find
**Players:** 6 or more

How fast could you walk if your feet were as big as Bigfoot's? Find out! Divide up into two teams, and the first player from each team should put a giant shoebox on each foot. Then he should run (or shuffle—you don't want to lose those shoeboxes!) to the end of the course and come back. First team to have all their players shuffle their way to the finish line wins.

# TOILET PAPER TOSS

**What You'll Need:** Two rolls of toilet paper
**Players:** 8 or more

Divide up into two teams, and then line up each team in two rows facing each other (everyone should have someone facing them *from their own team*). Make sure you and your teammates are standing equal distances apart from one another (the other team should be standing the same distance apart as well). First person from each team takes a toilet paper roll and throws it to the teammate who is directly across from him, *while holding on to an end*. That player catches it, grabs on to the toilet paper "line" and throws it to the next player across from her. See which team can get through the whole line first. **Don't worry if the toilet paper rips. Just grab on again, and keep throwing!**

# SOCK JUG

**What You'll Need:** Over-sized old socks, plastic cups, water, three buckets

**Players:** 6 or more

**WARNING:** If your ankles have a fear of water, then this is *not* the game for you! Your ankles are in? Great! This game is best played outside, so go out into the yard and set up one bucket filled with water at the start and two empty buckets (one for each team) at the finish line (wherever you decide). Then put on your over-sized socks (over your bare feet—you don't want shoes for this one!). On "go," the first person for each team should fill their cups with water and put one plastic cup inside each sock (next to the ankle). **The object of the race is to carry the most water back to your team's bucket using your ankles (no hands!).** Once the first player gets to the finish line, he should empty his cup into his team's bucket and run back so the next person can go. (Okay, fine—on the way back, he can carry the empty cups in his hands!) After everyone has gone, measure the water in the buckets to see which team's ankles lugged the most water in their sock jugs!

## BACKWARDS WADDLER

**What You'll Need:** Two basketballs, soccer balls, volleyballs, or any other large ball

**Players:** 6 or more

Divide up into two teams, and give one ball to each team. The first player should put the ball between his knees and try to walk as fast as he can to the end of the course and back—sound easy? There's a catch! You have to do it *backwards*! First team to have all their players waddle their way to the finish line wins.

# Switcheroo Ball

Who says that we always have to use a basketball to play basketball and a baseball to play baseball? How about pulling a switcheroo?

## Laundry Basket Beach Ball

**What You'll Need:** A laundry basket, beach ball
**Players:** 1 or more

You'll need one of those large, round laundry baskets for this game. **The basket has to be large enough for you to throw your beach ball into, because that's exactly what you'll be doing.** To play, put the laundry basket down in an open area 10 to 15 feet from where you'll be standing. Now take your beach ball, dribble for a couple of steps (that is, bounce the ball on the ground as you walk), and try to shoot it into the basket. Did it go in? Move the basket around to challenge yourself (like on top of a deck outside your house) and see how many times you can get it in!

**CHALLENGE:** Like playing under pressure? Grab a stopwatch and see how many baskets you can make in sixty seconds. Then try it with a friend. Who gets the most points in sixty seconds?

## Wiffle Bat Beach Ball Hockey

**What You'll Need:** Wiffle bats, beach ball, four cones/goals

**Players:** 4 or more

**How about using a wiffle bat as a hockey stick and playing a game of hockey with a beach ball?** Watch out! That's one big puck!

To play, first set up the goals. If you're using cones, set them up about 4 feet apart. You'll need two goals on opposite ends of wherever you're playing. Break up into two teams. Each team should pick a goalie—this is the player who tries to keep the puck (or the beach ball) from going through the goal. For everyone else the "goal" is to score a goal! Score a goal by hitting the puck (beach ball) with your hockey stick (wiffle bat) past the goalie on the opposite team! Remember, unless you're the goalie, no hands! Just use that wiffle ball bat and keep that ball on the ground! The team with the most points when time's up is the winner.

# On the Move—
# Games to Play on the Go

Whether you're in the car, a bus, or a plane, sometimes all you have to get there is a ticket to Boresville, if you know what we mean! But no worries! This chapter's jam-packed with stuff for you to do while you're out and about, or stuck someplace for a while. Read on!

## CAR GAMES

Yes! It's finally time to leave for vacation and you've been spending most of the past few days dreaming about your trip. You grab your bags, dash out of the house, and do a pretty impressive leap into the car—who knew you could clear the entire driveway in a single bound? You're psyched!

But how long does it take before *it* starts to happen?

You know: **the car suddenly feels like it's shrinking**. Your big (or little) sibling's leg creeps into your half of the back seat. You shift around, looking for a comfortable position, but can't find one. A horrible itchy feeling builds, as you shift and scratch, until finally you can't stand it anymore: *"Are we there yet?!"* you yell. *"How much further do we have to go?! How much longer until we get there?!"*

But fear not! You hold in your hands the secret to getting through any trip *without being bored!* Once you've made it through this section, instead of whining, you'll say *"Slow down, driver…no need to speed. I'm having a grand old time back here! In fact, once we get to the water park, you folks can go ahead without me, I'd rather stay in the car!"* Okay, maybe not, but let's just say you'll be having so much fun that passing cars will notice and wonder: *"What's going on in that car? Why are the kids in that back seat smiling? Are we there yet??"*

## EAGLE EYE

Staring blankly at the road with your face pressed up against the glass will only smudge your window and make a two-hour journey feel decades long! *"Is it me, or did I just celebrate another birthday during this road trip?"* Here's a game to make time fly!

**What You'll Need:** A set of good peepers (your eyes, that is), paper, pencil

**Players:** 2 or more

Create a list of things to look for, and compete with fellow passengers for the title of "Eagle Eye". **First, you and the other players create a list of things to look for—you can make your list as imaginative and wacky as you want.** You guys call the shots! Think of things that you might see outside the car (before, of course, you see them). Give the less challenging items a five-point value (police car, bridge, helicopter) and the more challenging items a ten-point value (pink car, flat tire, monkey—you never know!). The goal of the game is to be the first one to see any of the things on the list. If you do, call it, and those points are yours. One player should be the official scorekeeper (preferably someone with trustworthy math skills). The one who has the most points in the end has earned the title "Eagle Eye"!

**SUPER DUPER DOUBLE BONUS:** Anyone who spots a real eagle gets 20 points!

### Survival Tip

Remember that pictures of objects count too, so don't overlook billboards and bumper stickers!

# JINGLES

**What You'll Need:** Your imagination, a quick wit, the guts to belt out a tune
**Players:** 2 or more

Say the magic words *"My baloney has a first name…"* to anybody who knows the tune and you'll be amazed at what happens. As if controlled by an invisible hypnotist, he'll sing out: *"it's O-S-C-A-R…"* You might want to run for cover or have some earplugs handy, because it's very likely you'll hear the person sing out the jingle over and over again. The Oscar Mayer® ditty was written by some sneaky folks at Oscar Mayer years ago to stick in your brain the way a piece of chewed gum sticks to your shoe (if you're unlucky enough to step in it)!

These short, catchy tunes on commercials are called "jingles". Companies pay loads of loot to have crafty people write these tunes for them, because a good jingle is like a mini-salesperson in shoppers' ears constantly reminding them to buy.

**Ready to try and make up some sticky tunes?** Then you're ready to play Jingles! When it's your turn, spot the next billboard, advertisement, restaurant, or store you pass, and immediately belt out a jingle you know—or make one up. There's no time to break out the composition paper, and definitely not enough room in the back seat for a piano, so just relax and let the tune out of your mouth. Use your imagination! Don't worry if your jingle doesn't rhyme—it doesn't have to. And it can be in any musical style (country, rap, disco, opera), and as silly as you want. For extra fun, try singing in different voices. See who comes up with the catchiest jingles. And who knows? Maybe your tune will be so catchy that you'll convince your folks to take you to Big Dave's Pizza Palace for lunch, without even having to ask!

**VARIATION:** If you don't feel like belting out ads, how about trying to come up with a catchy slogan for them? Think of slogans that you may know, like *"Think Outside the Bun,"* and *"The Quicker Picker Upper."* Can you write one for a passing restaurant, amusement park, or store?

**ANOTHER VARIATION:** Think of your favorite jingles or slogans, and see who can be the first to guess what product they're for. Here are a few slogans to try: *"Just do it," "They're grrrrreat!," "Silly rabbit," "Gather 'round the good stuff".* See how many you can come up with. Can you stump everyone in the car?

## CAR-TIST

**What You'll Need:** A pad of paper, pencil
**Players:** Just you in a moving car

Is your car an artist? Have you ever seen any of its work? Who knows? **Your family van could really be a Van Gogh!** But before you consider replacing the windshield wipers with paintbrushes, try this: place your pad of paper comfortably on your lap. This will be the car's canvas. Now take your pencil and rest its tip lightly on the paper. Let your arm and wrist relax as the movement of the car carries the pencil across the paper. Try not to guide the pencil or put any pressure on it—this is your *car's* chance to express itself, *not* yours! Sometimes it helps to close your eyes, or put your head back on the head rest. After a fair amount of time, take a peek and check out your car's work. *Voilà!* Your car drew a picture! What do you think? Is it the next Mona Lisa?

## RED CAR, BLACK CAR

So you and your brother are starting to get that itchy feeling, and the back seat is shrinking faster than a snowball in July. You wish you had a measuring stick because you *know* you could prove it. Instead of yelling *"Ma, he's touching me again!"* for the twenty-five-hundredth time, challenge him to a game of Red Car, Black Car—and before you know it, the back seat will feel twice its original size!

**What You'll Need:** Your Checkers mini game, sharp eyes
**Players:** 2

**Imagine that your travel checkerboard is the wide open road.** Now use the checkers (red and black cars) to make a traffic jam. Crunch the cars together in the center of the board (think how angry those teeny tiny people driving them must be!). Each player should choose a color (red or black). The object of the game is to get all your cars to your side of the board. Each one is worth 1 point. How do you get them out of the jam? By spotting cars out the window that match your color! But be quick about it, because here's the twist: if you see your opponent's color whiz by before he does, you get to take one of his chips—yup, one of the ones in the jam. These are worth *2* points.

**The game is over when all the cars are cleared from the middle.** Now tally up your points. The player with the highest score is (you guessed it) the winner. Feel all that extra elbow room now? You totally forgot you were in the car, didn't you? Okay, maybe not…but you *did* manage to stop the incredible shrinking back seat—at least while playing this game!

## Make Your Own Scrapbox!

A scrapbook of your travels is a great way to remember your trip. But try thinking outside the box and make **a scrap*box*** instead! A box full of souvenirs and memorabilia is as much fun to make as it is to go through later. Before your trip, **find a medium-sized box with a lid** (a shoebox is perfect), and a rubber band or two large enough to keep it closed. (You want to *keep* the stuff you collect—not lose it!) **Collect business cards, napkins, brochures, ticket stubs, postcards** (they're not just to mail!), **rocks, shells,** and **other stuff** along your traveling way. You can also add little notes to remind yourself what those "scraps" mean to you (or even what they are, if need be). Get creative! The possibilities are endless. Always be on the lookout for things to put in your scrapbox and, when you get home, you'll remember the *whole* trip a whole lot more than you otherwise might—pit stops and all!

# FRIFFLEZOOTER

What is a *Frifflezooter*, you ask? The name of the game is figuring the Frifflezooter out!

**What You'll Need:** A sharp eye, the ability to say *"Frifflezooter"*
**Players:** 2 or more

The first player is the sneaky one who secretly picks out something that appears over and over again on the road (like a truck). Every time the sneaky first player sees the item he chose, he calls out, *"Frifflezooter!"* The other players have to guess what the word "Frifflezooter" stands for (in this case, a truck). The first person that guesses correctly gets to pick the next Frifflezooter!

## SNEAKY TIP

The "Frifflezooter" can also be something that's *happening in the car*—for example, whenever your brother scratches his nose. Or, you can make the Frifflezooter mean "anytime your brother asks a question". **CAUTION:** this has the potential to drive him nuts. See conversation below:

**YOUR BROTHER:** *I give up. What is it?*

**YOU:** *Frifflezooter.*

**YOUR BROTHER:** *Just tell me already. Is it air or something?*

**YOU:** *Frifflezooter.*

**YOUR BROTHER:** *Are you trying to drive me nuts?*

**YOU:** *Frifflezooter.*

Get the idea? *Frifflezooter.* No, what we mean is, do you really get what this game is all about? *Frifflezooter.* Okay, okay. You get it!

## PEPPERONI PIZZA

Getting hungry yet? Well, if your folks keep telling you they want to get through another twenty miles before stopping for lunch, play Pepperoni Pizza—and make them hungry *now*!

**What You'll Need:** Your Checkers mini game
**Players:** 2 or more

Make a giant circle on your checkerboard with the black checkers (well, as giant as you can make it on a mini board!). This is your pizza pie. Use all your red checkers to sprinkle pepperoni on top. Mmmm. All ready? Okay, stop drooling and **keep your eyes peeled on the road as you look for things that you can put on a pizza**. Every time you find something, say *"I like* (insert the thing you spotted here) *on my pizza"* and take a piece of the pizza (one checker, black or red, doesn't matter). The things you find don't necessarily have to be food, but you should be able to put it on top of a pizza and eat it. Sorry, but *"I like tires on my pizza"* wouldn't count. Unless you think you could fit it on a pizza pie and eat it, it's a no go. But that doesn't mean you can't get creative—if a fly passes by your nose, there'd be nothing wrong with saying *"I like flies on my pizza."* So grab a piece of pizza and keep going. And of course: no repeats. That'd be way too easy!

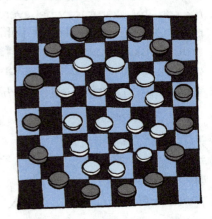

Once your pizza pie has disappeared, count up your pieces. The winner is the one who has the most checkers. So, did you manage to get your folks hungry—or just ruin their appetite?

### SNEAKY TIP

If the radio is on, use it! If you hear an ad for chicken, say, or a story about chocolate, or something else you can put on your pizza, claim it before the other players do!

## Be a Food Critic!

Going to restaurants and pit stops can be fun, and by taking note (literally), you'll notice a lot more than you did before. **Make a small notebook your "food journal"—and review all the places where you eat. You can give the places a rating for food, atmosphere, and service.** (You also just might keep folks on their toes—when they see a critic at the table, they want to provide their best!) Date the entry and provide your review of what you ate and how your meal and overall experience was. (If you have a camera, you can even take pictures to keep track of what you were served!) **Bonus:** If you ever go that way again, when everyone else is saying *"I think we ate there on our last trip, but I don't remember what it was like…"* you'll be able to whip out your notebook and provide your full critique and recommendation!

## LICENSE PLATE WORD STORM

Look out your window and what do you see? Yeah, there are other cars—but those aren't *just* cars whizzing by. They've got letters and words just waiting to be found! See how many words you can find in this game!

**What You'll Need:** Paper, pencil (one for each player)
**Players:** 1 or more

The first player writes down the car color and license plate letters of the first car that passes. Each player does the same with a different car that passes by. Now let the brainstorming begin! The goal is to make as many words as you can with the letters (from the license plate and the word of the color) that you got from the car you picked. Everyone should agree on a time limit beforehand. Players win 1 point for each word under four letters and 2 points for words four letters and up.

For example, say you got a blue car with a license plate that says CET423. From the letters in "blue" and "CET423" you could get the words "belt," "bee," and "cue"—that's 4 points right there! The player with the most points at the end of the round wins.

### BONUS ALERT!

If a player is crafty enough to use *all* their letters in a single word, they score 10 big bonus points.

**VARIATION:** Everyone plays with the same car's color and license plate. After the time's up, go over your words together. Cross off words that more than one player wrote down. The winner is the one who came up with the most words that nobody else thought of.

**VANITY VARIATION:** What would your license plate "say" if you could write it? Your name? Your nickname? Your favorite sport? Everyone in the car should design their own plate (seven letters or numbers max). Now trade vanity plates and see how many words you can storm up!

> ## Survival Tip
> Always be prepared—you never know when your folks will be up for a spontaneous trip to Aunt Rose's, so put together a **Car Survival Kit** and you'll be ready to go anytime. Put some stuff like paper, pencils, crayons, a journal, and your mini Checkers and Boggle (or this book!) in a bag and stash it somewhere in your car. It's always good to be prepared!

# STUCK!

The dictionary has three definitions for the word "stuck":

**1.** *jammed, caught, or held in a position from which it's impossible to move*

Yes, this is what we're talking about—being *stuck* in traffic, or even *stuck* in a waiting room, or worse...*stuck* shopping with your 'rents.

**2.** *not able to find a solution or way out of a situation*

This is definitely not the definition of *stuck* we're talking about—there *is* a solution to the boredom that takes over while you're *stuck*. (It's in the games on the following pages!)

**3.** *pierced by a sharp object*

This is also not the definition of *stuck* we're talking about. And we certainly hope this definition of *stuck* doesn't happen to you—ever. Yeowch!

It's bad enough when you're uncomfortable in the car, but now you're not even *moving*. These games are great for when you're stuck in traffic, stuck shopping, or stuck waiting. Just because you're *stuck* (definition 1) doesn't mean you have to be *stuck* (definition 2). So play these games and get un-stuck!

# THE FORBIDDEN WORD

**What You'll Need:** Your imagination and smarts
**Players:** 2 or more

You know that there are certain words you're not supposed to say—and no, we're not going to list them here! In this game, you get to choose the word that's forbidden—and then try and get someone *else* to say it.

The first player chooses a "forbidden word" and tells everyone else playing—except one person—what it is (if you're playing with only two players total, you should write it down). No one should use the "forbidden word"—after all, it's *forbidden*! **The object of the game is to get the person who doesn't know what the forbidden word is to say it.** "How am I supposed to do that?" you ask. Use your crafty noggin and take turns asking him questions. For example, if the forbidden word is "tricks," you might ask *"What does a magician do?"* or *"What do people do on April Fool's Day?"* The first person that gets him to say the forbidden word is the winner—and the winner gets to choose the next forbidden word.

**VARIATION:** Everyone in the car agrees on a forbidden word that's used frequently ("the" or "it"). Now it's every player for themselves! Try to get your opponents to say the forbidden word. But be careful! Make sure you don't use the forbidden word in your questions! You'll be surprised at how difficult it is to talk! When you've said the forbidden word, you're out, but there's no need to sit quietly. You can still try to get everyone else to say the forbidden word, and since you're already out, you can use it yourself. The last person standing is the big winner.

**VARIATION ON THE VARIATION:** Try the game with a forbidden letter. It's played the same way as the variation above, but uses a letter instead of a word. Stay on your toes! If the letter appears in any of the words you say, you're out.

## ONCE UPON A...

There was a...*what?* It's your turn, so you tell us! Looking for a little entertainment? Put everyone's heads together to tell a story, and get whisked off to a far-away land where Boredom just doesn't exist!

**What You'll Need:** Your imagination
**Players:** 2 or more

The game is simple: the first player starts off by saying the phrase *"Once upon a time...."* Then the next player says one word to add to the story. So the next person, for example, could say *"there,"* and each player keeps taking turns, adding one word until someone decides the tale is over and says *"The End."* The best way to play this game is to move quickly, so that you actually hear the story. So, try saying the first word (that makes some sort of sense) that pops into your brain. You never know what's going to happen next!

**VARIATION:** Instead of adding one word each, try adding a sentence each, to change it up. The first player can start off by saying something like *"Once upon a time, there was a boy with webbed feet."* And the next player could say something like *"His name was Cornelius Corncob."* Continue on until the story ends.

**VARIATION ON THE VARIATION:**
How about challenging yourself and trying to make your story rhyme? You can alternate and rhyme wherever you feel that you can. For example, if the first person said the example above, *"Once upon a time, there was a boy with webbed feet,"* the next player could say *"He loved to dance, but couldn't keep the beat."* Get it? Got it? Good. Don't wait—go create!

## MONKEY

Feeling sharp? Think you can make a monkey out of your co-travelers? Challenge them to a battle of the brains. Play the wild word game Monkey to see who ends up swinging from the rafters!

**What You'll Need:** Just you and your fast-thinking mind
**Players:** 2 or more

Someone has to go first—and it might as well be you! Choose a letter and say it out loud to your opponents. Let's just say you pick the letter "S". The next player says another letter out loud, but has to make sure that it could be the second letter in a word starting with the letter you chose. Let's say the second player chooses the letter "A". This would be a good choice because lots of words start with the letters "SA" (*say, safe, salami, salutation*). Now, the game gets more challenging as you go, because the next player has to say another letter, and so on, until a word is formed. But you *don't* want to be the one who forms the word. Why? Keep reading!

**The object of the game is to go on saying letters for as long as possible.** The player who completes the word loses that round and gets an "M". The next time he loses a round, he gets an "O". (See where we're going with this?) But hold it right there! There's another way to earn those dreaded letters. If a player adds a letter that the others don't think could be a word (like if he adds an "X" to an "S-A-L"), then you can call him on it and challenge him: *"Sorry buddy, but I don't think there's a word in the English language that starts with 'salx.' I hereby challenge you."* (Use "hereby" if you want to sound extra official!) If he's wearing his smarty pants and can come up with a word, then he wins the round and *everyone else* gets an "M".

If he *can't* come up with a word, he gets the "M". Play until someone gets all the letters in "MONKEY". Whoever has the fewest letters in the word "MONKEY" wins!

Make sure you all agree on a few rules before you begin. Can you use slang words? Is there a minimum length the word should be? Should you give the MONKEY a banana?

## GUM SCULPTURE

Feeling artistic? Longing to create something that you can call a work of art? Grab as much gum as you can get your hands on and make a gum sculpture!

**What You'll Need:** Lots o' gum
**Players:** Just you and your choppers

Once you get your hands on some gum, start chewing! Don't go too crazy—make sure you can still close your mouth! Now blow a bubble. It should be pretty big, so you might want to warn your mom to watch the back of her head! Once you blow your bubble, close the end of it with your tongue to keep the air in, and carefully take it out of your mouth. Now stretch and pull it to sculpt it into any shape you want. Can you make a baseball bat or a butterfly? How about some underpants?

## Survival Tip

**HANDLE WITH CAUTION:** Your art is gooey—and the family car (and just about everything else) is probably very anti-goo. Try not to let the two come in contact! And be sure to get permission first. If not, it could make your time spent stuck a whole lot stickier—for you!

# All Hands on Deck—Card Games

Tired of playing the same old card games over and over? Well, don't throw away that card deck just yet! Grab some friends (or just yourself) and find a comfy place to park it. You'll want to play these games—again and again!

## Survival Tip

Generally, if you have six or more players, you should play with two decks of cards. And be sure to take the jokers out of the deck!

### I DOUBT IT!

Liars abound in this game! See if you know who's telling the truth, but be careful about who you doubt—if you're wrong, you'll have to pay!

**What You'll Need:** A deck of cards
**Players:** 4 or more

Shuffle and deal the cards out one at a time until all of the deck is used up and everyone has the same number of cards. (If there are some cards left over, just put them face down in the middle of the table.) **The first player starts off by putting down aces—or at least he *says* he's putting down aces**. He takes a number of cards from his hand and places them face down in the center of the table, while announcing what they are. So if he puts down three cards, he'd say *"Three aces."* The cards are put in the center in number order, so the next player should put down a two (or twos) and so on, up through kings. (After kings, start at aces again.)

**Remember, cards are put *face down* in the center of the table, so you can never be sure if someone's putting down what he says he put down.** And there's the catch: if you don't believe that first player put down three aces, you can say *"I doubt it!"* Once you've said it, turn over the cards that the first player laid down. If he was a dirty rotten liar and *did not* put down three aces, he must take *all* the cards in the center. *But* if he was honest and *did* put down three aces, *you* have to take all the cards in the center. The player to get rid of all his cards first wins.

## Survival Tip

Pay attention to the cards you have in your hand and remember that there are only four cards to each number or face card (jacks, queens, and kings) in one deck. If a player puts down three cards and declares, *"Three threes"* and you see that you have two threes in your hand, you know he's fibbing—speak up and doubt him!

**SNEAKY TIP:** Do you see a pattern? Can you tell when your friend is lying because of the way she twirls her hair or shifts her eyes when she's nervous? Does your brother get a funny twisted smile on his face when he claims he's putting down aces but really isn't? Be on the lookout for any signs, and you'll get better at figuring out when players are lying (or when they're telling the truth)!

**SUPER SNEAKY TIP:** Some players wear sunglasses to hide their eyes so their peepers don't give them away!

## SNAP!

**What You'll Need:** A deck of cards
**Players:** 2 or more

Deal out the deck of cards until you run out. (It's okay if the cards aren't distributed equally.) Each player puts her stack of cards face down in front of her. Now, take turns putting one card face up beside your stack (so you should have two piles—one face up and one face down). No peeking before you flip, please! When someone flips a card that matches a card in someone else's face-up pile (by number or face), the first player to call out *"Snap!"* wins the stacks with the matching cards and adds them to the bottom of her own pile.

But be careful about blurting out *"snap,"* because if you're mistaken, then *you* have to give the other players *one card* from your stash. Once you've flipped all your cards, turn over your face-up stack (so now it's face down) to continue playing. The first player to get all of the cards wins.

**VARIATION:** Get speedy! Everyone puts out cards at the same time instead of taking turns. Watch out! It's bound to get LOUD!

## MY SHIP SAILS

**What You'll Need:**
A deck of cards
**Players:** 4 or more

The dealer shuffles the cards and deals out seven cards to each player (and lays the rest of the deck aside). Hold your cards and arrange them into suits (the suit is the symbol on the card: hearts, diamonds, clubs, or spades). The object of the game is to collect seven cards of the same suit, so decide which suit you will collect—but don't get too attached, you might have to change in the middle of the game! Every player should choose a card that he doesn't want and pass it (face down) to the player on his left. Then, all the players should pick up the card that their neighbors handed to them. Keep passing and picking up cards until someone gets a full hand of the same suit. The first person to have seven cards of the same suit shouts *"My ship sails!"* and is the winner.

## STEAL THE BUNDLE

**What You'll Need:** A deck of cards
**Players:** 2

Shuffle the cards and deal four to yourself and four to your opponent—face down. Deal four more cards face up in the middle of the table. Your opponent should go first. If he has a card that matches rank (the number or the face) with one of the cards in the center, he can take that card and the matching card from his hand, and put it face up in a second pile next to him. This is his "bundle". If he doesn't have a matching card, he puts a card from his hand face up in the middle.

Now the game gets more interesting. It's your turn. If you have a card that matches a card in the center, you can capture it and put it in your bundle. *But,* if you have a card that matches the face-up card in your opponent's bundle, you can "steal" his bundle and add it to your own. If nothing matches, take one card from your hand and lay it next to the cards in the middle.

**A RULE:** You have to add cards to your "bundle" in the order in which they're captured—so you should add the cards to the *top* of your bundle only.

**ANOTHER RULE:** In any one turn, you can capture as many cards from the table cards as you have matching cards in your hand.

When you run out of cards, deal out another four. No cards get added to the middle. Keep playing until all the cards have been dealt and played. The player with the most cards in his bundle wins!

# Solo Card Games (Just For You!)
## Pyramid

**What You'll Need:** A deck of cards
**Players:** Just you

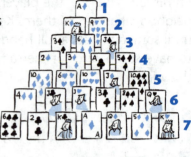

Shuffle the cards and deal out 28 of them, face up, in 7 rows to form a pyramid. Start at the top with one card in the first row, then put down two cards for the second row, overlapping the bottom of the first row. Lay three cards down for the third row, overlapping with the second, and keep laying down

HAND

TALON

DISCARD

cards in rows, adding one card per row and overlapping the bottom of the row above it, until you get to the seventh row. All the cards in rows 1–6 should have two cards overlapping the bottom edge. (If you're having trouble setting up, take a look at the picture for help.) Once you've made your pyramid, put the rest of the deck in a stack face down in front of you, on the left side. This is your "Hand" pile.

All set up? Good. Now look at the bottom row of cards in the pyramid. Since these cards don't have any other cards lying on top of them, they're "free" cards. **Can you add the values of any two cards in that row to make 13?** (Note: a Jack counts for 11, a Queen 12, a King 13, and an Ace 1.) If you can, pick up those two cards and put them in a pile on your right—this is your "Discard" pile. If there are any other free cards in the row that add up to 13, put them in your Discard pile—if not, turn over the top card in your Hand pile (the cards on your left side). Can you add its value to any of the cards on the bottom row of the pyramid to get 13? If you can make 13, pick up both cards (the one from your Hand pile and the one from the bottom row of the pyramid) and put them in your Discard pile.

If you can't use the top card in your Hand pile to make 13, put it face up in the middle below the pyramid. This is the "Talon" pile. So now there are three possible piles you can have: the "Hand," the "Discard," and the "Talon" pile. Let's go over these piles, just to be clear. In front of you on your left side, face down, you have the mysterious "Hand" pile. These are the cards you're turning over to match up with another card in the pyramid to make 13. In the middle, you have the lovely "Talon" pile. These are the cards that you haven't been able to use yet, but don't worry, you'll get another chance. Then on the right side, last but certainly not least, is the glorious "Discard" pile. These are the gems that you've already used to make 13, and are done with. Got it? Good!

Okay, let's get back to the game. For your next move, you've got new options. **Now you can turn over another card from your Hand pile and use it to try to get 13,** *or* **you can use the card that is face up on top of the Talon pile.** Remember: you're trying to use one of these cards to add to a free card in the pyramid to get 13. You can also pair up cards in the pyramid that are free (that aren't blocked by any cards overlapping them) and put them in your Discard pile at any point in the game. **The game is over when the Hand pile is gone and all possible combinations of 13 have been made.** If you've cleared away the entire pyramid, you've won!

**RULE TO REMEMBER:** When a King pops up in your Hand pile or becomes free in the pyramid, you can happily throw him right on the Discard pile—because kings are worth 13!

## SPEED SOLITAIRE

**What You'll Need:** A deck of cards, stopwatch
**Players:** Just you

You'll need a stopwatch for this fast-moving game to race yourself against the clock. The goal is to (quickly) complete each suit. Place four cards, each of a different suit, face up in front of you (it doesn't matter what number they are, just as long as there's one card of each suit). These are the cards you'll be building on. Now it's time to speed! Deal out four cards at a time (face up) and quickly match them to their suit. Go through all the cards and see how fast you can go. Don't forget to start the stopwatch!

# Magic Tricks—Now You See It, Now You Don't

**B**oredom is bad enough, but what do you do when its horrible and nasty relative pays a visit? The dreaded "Blahs" can hit you when you least expect it. There's no explanation for it—you just don't feel like doing *anything*. You feel more like a sloth than a kid—and you wonder if you should just call it a day and go hang from some branches in your yard….

**Stop right there!** *Don't do it!* Don't resort to living on leaves and 18 hours of sleep a day! There *is* a way to get rid of those blahs and all it takes is a few magic words!

It's true. **Magic is the perfect way to chase away your inner sloth and bust through those blues.** In this section, you'll learn some really **cool tricks** that are fun to do and, on top of that, they'll **shock and amaze your friends**! (Sloths don't get to do that!)

Most of what you need for these tricks, you probably have in your house right now, so what are you waiting for? Say some magic words and then shout *"Boredom Blahs be gone!"*

## First, a Word on those Magic Words…

*Hocus pocus? Presto chango? Abracadabra?* Come on! You don't have to use the same old words for *your* magic. **Make up your own!** It could be **a word, a phrase, or even a song**—anything you want. How about *"Kalamazoo!"* or *"Turkey Jerky Chicken Burger!"*? What about inventing your own word, like *"Piggahantis!"*? Think about it and come up with a bunch of your own. Try them out and see which works best for you!

## ONE MORE THING BEFORE WE START...

Every good magician comes prepared—the trick just wouldn't be the same if we saw the magician setting up all his equipment before the show, would it? **Preparing beforehand** (or "prepping" if you want to sound like a pro) **allows you to do your sneaky work behind closed doors.** This way, the audience stays totally clueless—just the way you want it!

## PAPER CLIPPED

You probably have tons of paper clips sitting around your house. And what does everyone use them for? Clipping paper together? How boring! That can't be fun for them *or you*! Snag some of those bored paper clips and get ready to impress your friends with this very cool trick.

**What You'll Need:** A $1 bill, paper clips

**Prep Time:** Fold a $1 bill into thirds. Fold the right third toward the back and the left third toward the front so that it looks like a Z. Got it? Good. Now put one paper clip on the left side, making sure you clip the back and middle sections of the dollar only. Put the next two clips to the right of that and clip together just the middle and the front sections. Easy enough, right?

**Show Time:** Tell the audience that you're about to link up the paper clips without ever touching them. Then say something like *"Hear ye, hear ye! Paper clips before me, listen up. You will link up on my command!"* (Put on a real serious face when you say this for full effect.) Hold the ends of the dollar in each hand and say *"My command!"* as you quickly pull on both ends of the bill. The dollar will straighten out and send a chain of paper clips flying through the air!

### SLICK TIP

For an extra touch of pizzazz, practice catching the paper clip chain on its way down. *Slick!*

**NEVER-ENDING VARIATION:** Once you have a chain, fold up your dollar bill and do it again! Use one clip from the chain and two additional clips to set it up the same as you did before. You can do the trick again and again (adding clips each time) and they'll continue to link up. Try different sizes and colors. They'll all work! Pretty cool, huh?

## TORN PHOTO

The audience watches nervously as a photo gets torn to shreds. You say a few magic words and…it's perfectly restored!

**What You'll Need:** Two duplicate photos, two envelopes, glue, scarf

**Prep Time:** First, you have to build a sneaky envelope. Glue two plain white envelopes together back-to-back so that the flaps are facing out. You want the audience to believe that this is just a regular old innocent envelope, so make sure it looks like that's all it is! Check those corners out—you want them to be glued together tightly, so there are no suspicious edges sticking up!

Two envelopes glued together

### Survival Tip

For glue, try using a glue stick. It works perfectly for this trick. No puckering or glue marks to give it away!

Once you have your sneaky envelope together, you have one last thing to prep: put one of the photos inside one of the envelopes and seal it. Simple enough, right?

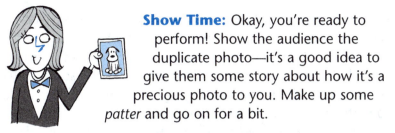

**Show Time:** Okay, you're ready to perform! Show the audience the duplicate photo—it's a good idea to give them some story about how it's a precious photo to you. Make up some *patter* and go on for a bit.

### JARGON ALERT!

*Patter* is a magician's word for the chatter you say to the audience while performing a trick. This talk can entertain, add suspense, and, more importantly, distract your audience when you're doing something fishy right under their clueless noses!

Okay, back to the trick. Tell the audience you need a volunteer to come up and help you out by destroying the photo. Tell them that you will then restore it to it's perfect original condition. If you want to add some drama, say something like *"Well, that's what's supposed to happen. This is my first time doing this trick, and now I'm wondering if I should have practiced or something. If it doesn't work my mom will be pretty mad…"* Then tell the volunteer that he can destroy the photo and rip it up as many times as he wants—he'll probably have fun with this one!

Now show your audience the envelope with the unsealed side facing out. (Yes, this is your sneaky envelope, but make sure *they* can't tell!) Say something like *"I will now place the sad remains of this dear, dear photo of mine into this envelope."* Take the pieces of the shredded photo and drop them into the envelope. If you want to add some patter, look at the volunteer, and say something like *"Man, you really ripped this thing up! I'd hate to get on your bad side!"* Seal the envelope, but make sure you don't show the audience the back—otherwise, the jig is up! Cover it with your hand, or bend the flap backwards to lick, then paste it down.

Here comes the extra-super sneaky part: cover the envelope

with the scarf and carefully turn it around, so that the envelope you sealed earlier (the one with the good photo) is facing out. Even though you're maneuvering things under the scarf, as always, it's a good idea to cover the flip of the envelope with some patter, to distract your audience while you do your dirty work! You could say something like *"Does anyone have any tape in case this doesn't work? I have to say, I'm a little nervous! Well, here goes nothing!"*

Now put on your serious face and wave your hands, as you say something like *"Photograph, photograph all ripped and torn, I command you to return to your original form!"* Say your personal magic words as you whip away the scarf. As the audience holds their breath, slowly open the envelope and breathe a sigh of relief as you take out the perfectly restored photo for all to see. They'll be trying to figure that one out for weeks!

Audience View

## PARTING THE PEPPER

**What You'll Need:** Black pepper flakes, bowl of water, dish soap

**Prep Time:** Fill a bowl with water and sprinkle some black pepper on top. Put a sneaky dab of dish soap on your fingertip and you're ready to go!

**Show Time:** Challenge your friends to try and part the pepper with their finger. They can try and try, but the pepper will just sit there, staring at them. When you put your finger in, however, the pepper flees at your command! Try it and see. It's quick and easy fun!

**BEFORE**     **AFTER**

# MAGIC CUP-O-WATER

Watch jaws drop as you produce a bone-dry tissue from a cup *after* filling it with water!

**What You'll Need:** Two 16 oz. paper or plastic cups, two 5 oz. paper or plastic cups (just make sure the cups aren't see-through), clear packing tape, two tissues, cup of water

**Prep Time:** Take your two large cups and securely tape the two small cups inside the bottom of each one. To do that for each cup, make a small loop of tape and stick it to the side of the small cup. Put the small cup into the large cup, and stick it to the wall of the large cup, as far down in the large cup as possible. To secure it even more, use another piece of tape to stick the mouth of the inner cup to the wall of the outer cup. Make sure you can hold the large cups upside-down without the small ones falling out—if not, add more tape. These are going to be your "secret weapons," so you want them to *stay secret*! Also, make sure your audience won't be able to see inside your cups from where they're sitting—it's a secret, remember?

**Show Time:** All prepared? Good! Take out two dry tissues and tell the audience something like *"I will pour water into this cup, yet the tissue will emerge dry as a bone!"* Put one tissue into each cup—the inner cups, that is.

Once the tissues are in, pour some water into one of the large outer cups and say something like *"Hmm. This is going to be tough. This water's pretty wet!"* (Psst! Be careful while you're pouring that water! Remember not to splash any into the inner cup! After that, pour the water slowly from the first large cup into the other one (watch that tissue). Try to be natural when pouring the water, and always cover your sneaky actions with lots of patter to distract your audience. You could say something like *"Listen, folks, I know I claimed it'd be dry as a bone, but would you take dry as a day-old cucumber instead? You know—maybe just a little bit of water? This water is just so darn wet! No? Okay, okay, then. I'll see what I can do. It was worth a shot."*

OUTER CUP

Say some magic words, wave your hands, and pull the dry tissue out of the first cup...dry as a bone! Your audience will be shocked! Now for the double whammo: pull the dry tissue out of the second cup and watch as they look on in awe!

## Survival Tip

If you want to add some extra drama to this trick, when you're preparing your cups, put a tissue in one of the large cups—outside the small cup. This way, after you pour the water into the cup, you can show the audience a very wet, soggy, and gross tissue. You'll still have the dry one inside the other cup to show them after you say the magic words!

### THE UNSTOPPABLE, UNPOPPABLE BALLOON

Everyone knows if you stick a balloon with a pin, it'll pop—not to mention, make you jump! Then why doesn't yours?

**What You'll Need:** Balloons, transparent tape, pins

**Prep Time:** Blow up some balloons, but don't fill them up all the way, otherwise the trick won't work. Put a small piece of tape on your balloon. Make sure to rub the tape spot so it's as clear as it can look and keep it facing the balloon's back—you don't want your audience to see the tape!

**Show Time:** Hand out balloons to everyone and say something like *"I am about to shock and amaze you all. I can stick a balloon with a pin and it won't pop. In fact, it won't even make a peep!"* They probably won't believe you—and why should they? Pass out some pins and challenge them to try. If any of them are up for it, cover your ears, it'll probably get pretty loud! Then when you have everyone's attention, say a few magic words (and try not to flinch!) and stick *your* balloon with the pin (through the tape)...the balloon doesn't make a peep!

But don't take the pin out— there's no magic we know to keep a balloon with a hole in it inflated!

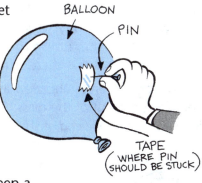

## Survival Tip

If you want to exaggerate this trick, and show off even more, you can hide several pieces of small tape on the balloon and stick it in more than one place—it's a balloon pincushion!

## ICE (CUBE) FISHING

You've heard of ice fishing, but ever heard of ice *cube* fishing? Challenge your friends to try and catch an ice cube from a glass of water using only the end of a string. Can they do it? Certainly not! But when *you* wave your hands over the glass and say a few magical words, what happens? You lift the ice cube right out of the water!

**What You'll Need:** A glass of water with ice, thin string (from a tea bag is best), salt

**Prep Time:** Fill a glass with water and some ice and get a short piece of string. The string from a tea bag works perfectly for this trick. Just rip the tea bag off and hold the string by the tab— instant fishing pole! Wet your string with a little water, so that it'll stick to the ice cubes better. There's one more very important thing to prepare before show time: hide some salt in the palm of your hand (about a tablespoon) and you're ready to fish!

**Show Time:** Set your glass of water and ice out. Now put the string in the glass like you're fishing. Start off by saying something like *"I've been fishing for ice cubes forever. Last year I caught a real*

*feisty one. He put up quite a fight—had to be this big."* (Make a big gesture with your hands.) *"Anyway, it's not easy because the ice cubes are pretty fussy. It's all in the wrist, really. Anyone care to give it a whirl? It looks like they're really jumping today!"*

Now sit back and enjoy the view as a volunteer tries to lasso or lift the ice cubes out of the glass. Remind him that ice cube fishing is done with only *one end* of the string, and he'll probably give up pretty quick. Now it's time for *you* to show your audience how it's done!

Lay one end of the string on the ice, wave your hands over the glass, and say some magic words. As you're waving your hands over the glass, slyly sprinkle the salt hidden in your palm onto the ice (don't make it obvious, but get a good amount on there). You want the string to sit for a moment after you put the salt on the ice so that it has time to cling. (Practice beforehand to get the timing just right.) So, as usual, it's a good idea to use some patter here to distract your audience, while you're waiting for the string to "catch on" to the ice. You could say something like *"Ooh, I just had a bite! Wait a minute… I think I got him. He's a big one all right!"* Then lift the string— you've made the catch of the day!

**CHALLENGE YOURSELF:** Try laying the string over more than one cube and see how many you can catch at once. Just make sure the string sits on the cubes you want (and the salt hits them all), and you might catch a tripler!

**THE SCIENCE OF IT:** Salt lowers the freezing point of the ice, making it melt enough for the string to stick to it when the ice refreezes.

## MUMMY FINGER

Tell your friend you got a mystery package in the mail. When you open it up to show him, there's a mummy finger in there! *Ahhhh!*

**What You'll Need:** A small square box with a lid (a cardboard jewelry box is perfect), paint, paintbrushes, cotton balls, baby powder

**Prep Time:** First, take your box and use paint to make it look old and creepy. Imagine what a box containing a mummy finger would look like. Would it be painted gold and have elaborate designs on it? Or would it look dusty and grimy? Design your box however you like. If you want, after the paint is dry, you can rough it up a bit by rubbing it in some dirt to make it look like it was dug up from the ground!

Next, cut a small hole in the bottom of it so you can stick your middle finger through it. Dust some baby powder on your finger for the full ancient-mummy effect. Pull apart some cotton balls and put them in the box so that when you put your finger in, you can't see the hole in the bottom. Put the lid on the box. When you open it, you might surprise yourself!

**Show Time:** Show your friend the box, keeping it angled downward—you don't want him to see that hole! Say something like *"I got a really strange package the other day. It came all the way from Egypt! I don't know anyone in Egypt. I haven't opened it yet because I'm kind of nervous. Should we look together?"* Now watch his face as you open the box to reveal a finger! He touches it and it moves!! Your friend screams, you scream. Quick! Close the box!

## PET ELEPHANT

Claim you have a pet elephant that you can produce from thin air. Go ahead and say it—you're about to do it...well, sort of!

**What You'll Need:** Tape, peanuts, small (aspirin-size) bottle, newspaper sheets

**Prep Time:** First, take out a sheet of newspaper and the bottle. Discard the bottle cap—you won't need it—and fill the bottle with some peanuts. Then lay the bottle on its side and tape it to the lower left-hand corner of the paper. Take a few extra sheets of newspaper to put on top of your sneaky secret one. Now you're ready to go!

**Show Time:** Start by saying something like *"Folks, I hope no one's allergic to elephants because I'm about to call my friend Zeke over to come and pay us a visit. Yup, that's right, Zeke's an elephant. Anyone allergic? No? Okay, good."* Grab your newspaper sheets (so that the one that you prepped is on the bottom of the stack) and hold up the papers so the bottle remains concealed from the audience's view. Say something like *"Zeke's not a front door kind of guy. He feels more comfortable coming through this magic door I create in the newspaper. Watch closely!"* Now roll up the paper (around the secret bottle) so that it looks like you're making a cone. (Don't do it too tightly—your peanuts will have a hard time escaping the bottle!) And remember to always cover your action with lots of patter. You can say something like *"Just to warn you guys: he's pretty huge. But don't worry! Zeke's a sweetheart."*

*Just try and make a little room when you see him coming. And try and duck if he sneezes—it can get pretty sloppy!"*

Now say the magic words and look into the newspaper cone like you're looking for the elephant. Tell the audience something like *"I can see him! Make room—here he comes!"*

Tip the cone as if you were going to release an elephant, and let the peanuts pour out. (Again, make sure the audience doesn't see that secret bottle!) Now say something like *"Oh, man! Guess he had to run before finishing his lunch!"* Watch your audience go wild!

## MY LOOSE THUMB

Tell a friend your thumb has been feeling loose. Watch her squirm when she tries to "tighten" it and actually turns it all the way around!

**What You'll Need:** A carrot, handkerchief

**Prep Time:** First, find a carrot that's about the same thickness as your thumb, and break it off so that it's a little longer than the length of your thumb. This will be your "dummy thumb". Hide your real thumb under your fingers to make a fist and hold the carrot to make it look like a thumb. Now cover your hand with a handkerchief. The carrot should look like your thumb from outside the handkerchief. Pretty slick, huh?

**Show Time:** Here comes the fun part! You're ready to tell someone that your thumb has been feeling "loose" lately. Ask her if she thinks she could help tighten it. She'll probably look at you like your head is full of walnuts, but go with it! Insist that all your thumb needs is a little twisting to "pop" it right back into place. Ham it up, and use those patter skills!

She's game? Good! Now have the poor sap hold onto your "thumb" (over the handkerchief, of course) and give it a few twists. Inevitably, she will look very disturbed as she feels your "thumb" (really the carrot!) twist around and around. Here comes the grand finale (and a chance to show off your acting skills!): while she's twisting, act like you're about to let out a gigantic sneeze. Turn and pull your hand out from under the handkerchief (thumb tucked under your fist) to cover your mouth as you sneeze. Your friend will be totally freaked out when she's left holding your thumb!

### ONE LAST TIP

We all know that practice makes perfect. It's a good idea to practice all these tricks in front of a mirror before performing them. Practice until you fool yourself—and you'll be ready to fool all your friends! What could be less boring than that?!

# Use Your Head— Games to Tease Your Brain

If you and a friend were stranded on a desert island, what would you do for fun? With no TVs, DVD players, video games, or sports equipment, do you think you'd go batty with boredom? Think once you got sick of shimmying up palm trees and tossing coconuts, there'd be nothing to do? **No matter where you are, or what's around you, there are *always* tons of fun things to do.** And that's because **you *always* have one incredible, amazing, marvelous, fun, and fantastic thing with you (*even* on a desert island): your brain.** Using your noggin's extraordinary power to figure things out is not only a way to give it a workout and let it strut its stuff, it's also loads of fun! So get going and see if you can boot Boredom right off your desert island!

## MIND GAMES

You already have what you need to play: your mind—and a couple of friends will come in handy, too.

### UNCLE ELMER

Uncle Elmer really is a strange old guy. What's his deal? That's what you have to figure out!

**What You Need:** Just your brain
**Players:** 2 or more

Uncle Elmer's so fussy. He has tons of rules about things he likes and dislikes. Who can keep track of them all? The first player gets to secretly decide something about Uncle Elmer that makes him a big weirdo. Does he only like things that are red? Does he hate words with "e" in them? Perhaps he can't stand plural words. How does he feel about things that are made of glass?

65

Once you have your rule, give clues—one at a time—to the other players and let them try and guess what it is about Uncle Elmer that makes him so odd. For example, if the rule you came up with was *"Uncle Elmer doesn't like things that fly,"* you could give a clue like *"Uncle Elmer hates bees and loves worms."* Your next clue could be *"Uncle Elmer won't travel by plane, and always takes the train."* Another could be *"Uncle Elmer hates birds, but loves birdseed."* The person who guesses your rule gets to talk about crazy old Uncle Elmer next!

## SUPER SLEUTH

Great detectives do more than dust for fingerprints and look good in trench coats—they take note of every last detail. Do you think you have what it takes to be a Super Sleuth? Try this game and find out!

**What You'll Need:** Just your brain
**Players:** 2 or more

You and a friend take turns being the "sleuth" and the "suspect". The first player to be the sleuth studies the suspect carefully. It helps to ask yourself questions like: *how is the suspect dressed? Is his shirt tucked in? What does his hair look like? Is he wearing a hat? Shoes? Socks?* Try and make a mental picture of every last detail about how he looks. Once the sleuth is ready to try and detect, she should close her eyes and turn away from the suspect—no peeking! **While the sleuth's eyes are shut, the suspect makes one small change to his appearance**—he could untie a shoe, roll down a sock, or even turn a hat slightly so it faces sideways…any little thing will do—as long as it's a change. When the

suspect's finished making the change to how he looks, it's time for the sleuth to go to work. **Can she figure out what's different?** Maybe the suspect put his shoes on the wrong feet. Or maybe he took his watch off. Was he wearing socks before? Give the sleuth a few guesses to get it right, then switch roles and let the suspect be the sleuth.

**VARIATION:** Instead of the suspect changing something about his appearance, he changes something about his surroundings. Did the suspect move the cookie jar from the kitchen counter and place it above the fridge? Did he turn the couch pillows around in the family room (or take one away)? Wasn't that backpack sitting on the piano stool before? Was the baseball mitt on the beanbag chair earlier? Try it out, Super Sleuth!

## INVENTION GRAB BAG

Ever wonder how people come up with inventions? Brainstorming is a good bet! You and your friends toss words together and come up with some inventions of your own with this game!

**What You'll Need:** Paper, pencils (one for each player), paper bag
**Players:** 2 or more

Each of the players should think of 10 objects and write them down on little slips of paper. Once that's done, it's time to head to the lab, or in this case—your paper bag! Fold up the slips of paper and put them in the bag. Shake the words around.

**Now pick two slips of paper out at a time. How do they go together? Do they give you an idea for an invention?** For example, if you picked the word *"helicopter"* and the word *"oven,"* together they could make, say, an *"ovencopter"*. What would that be? How would it work? What would it look like? Would an ovencopter zoom about on propellers? Would it fly around the house while it cooked up some mean mac and cheese?

Could you take the ovencopter out for a ride? (Or would you have to wait until you turned 18?) Sketch pictures of your favorite inventions (and also see **"It's Not Junk, It's My Invention!"** on page 79). Who knows—maybe they'll become the original plans for something big!

## PASS IT ALONG

Think you can communicate without speaking? How are your acting skills? See how well you and your friends do when you try "passing along" imaginary items!

**What You'll Need:** Your imagination
**Players:** 4 or more

**WARNING:** There will be heavy lifting in this game—and some of the things you have to lift could be slimy, greasy, or even stinky!
**THE GOOD NEWS:** The items are all *imaginary*! So even though they may weigh two tons, have moving wheels, or two sets of gigantic teeth that bite, at least you won't *really* feel the effects. You just have to *pretend* that you do!

First, break up into two teams. **The first team should form a huddle to come up with an imaginary object that they will pass along.** Will it be a mobile home? A dirty diaper? How about a bumblebee? A hot potato? Make your object as outrageous as you want it to be. Usually, the wackier it is, the more fun it will be to pass along!

Okay, now that the team has chosen an object, the first player pretends to pick it up (using exaggerated motions, of course), and passes it to the next player. The next player pretends to take it from the first player and passes it on down the line. This continues until you get to the last person on your team.

Now it's time for the other team to guess what your object is. If they can't figure it out, *pass it along again* to give them another chance—*this time with feeling*! Give them three or four chances to guess. Really get into it and try to perfect your performance. If they still can't get it, reveal the object, and then the other team goes, so it's your team's turn to guess.

## Survival Tip

When pretending to lift and pass along your object, try and imagine that you're *really* doing it. Think about the weight and size of the object. Does it bite? Is it gooey? Does it try to jump out of your hand? Use your imagination to help you with a convincing performance and you might even trick *yourself* into believing that you're really carrying that object!

# TOPSY TURVY DAY

Better warn everyone when it's coming—on Topsy Turvy Day, everything's turned around!

**What You'll Need:** Just your brain

Give your brain a whirl by trying to live life *upside down* and *backward* from what you're used to. Not to worry, you won't need to walk on the ceiling or anything...but if you figure out a way to do it, Topsy Turvy Day's definitely the time to show that skill off!

**Topsy Turvy is a day that you and your friends pick to do everything *upside down* and *backward*.** Just think of all the things you'd have to do differently when upside down is right side up, and backward is forward! It can get pretty confusing, so you should probably plan ahead!

Let's see...you'd definitely walk backward instead of forward—that's a no-brainer. You could start your day with a nice slice of pizza or a hamburger for breakfast. Save the pancakes or French toast for dinner! When

you get dressed, everything should go on backward and inside out—you could even try wearing your socks and sneakers on your hands—but that could get sweaty (not to mention stinky)! Whenever someone asks you a question on Topsy Turvy Day, you'd say *"yes"* when you mean *"no"* and *"no"* when you mean *"yes"*. This could definitely get confusing!

## PERFECT GAMES FOR TOPSY TURVY DAY
### EEB DRAWKCAB (OR BACKWARD BEE)
**What You'll Need:** Just your brain
**Players:** 2 or more

This game is like a spelling bee—except more fun because there's an upside-down twist: **when you get your word, you have to spell it backward!** If your opponent asked you to spell "*lamp*," how long would it take you to say *"P-M-A-L. Lamp"*? No writing it down!! Take turns and see who's the best backward speller.

**VARIATION:** Topsy Turvy it! Spell a word backward, then see how quickly your opponent can tell you what the word is!

### BACKTALK
**What You'll Need:** Just your brain
**Players:** 3 or more

If it's Topsy Turvy Day, you have to talk backward! Think of a word. Now try and say it backward! Can you use the word in a sentence? Try and see who can guess what the word is first. For example, if your word is, "potatoes," you could say, "*Seotatop. I love mashed seotatop!*"

## Some Other Opposite Ideas

- Say *"goodbye"* when you pick up the phone or see someone for the first time, and *"hello"* when you leave.
- Sing a song *backward*.
- Wear your sunglasses on the *back* of your head.

- Give your dog a cookie *and then* make him sit.
- Read a book from *end* to *beginning*.
- Wear your backpack as a *front*pack.

- Eat *under* the dining table.
- Write with your opposite hand.
- Sit backward in your chair (it might be tough to watch TV though!).
- Write a letter to your friend backward.
- Walk your dog backward (if he'll let you!).

Use your brainstorming skills to come up with more ideas, so you're totally prepared to do everything topsy turvy!

**P.S.** It might be best to try out Topsy Turvy Day on a weekend, or at home after school. Your teachers might have a hard time grading your tests if you list the answers backward!

### Things on Topsy Turvy Day That Wouldn't Change One Bit

There are some things on this wacky, backward, upside-down day that won't change at all! Anything that reads the same backward or forward is called a "palindrome". Words like *eye*, *racecar*, *level*, *peep*, and *wow* are all examples of palindromes. See how if you spell them backward they read the same forward? Weird, huh?

**Believe it or not, there are even whole sentences that are palindromes!** Write the letters in these sentences out backward and see for yourself!

"Never odd or even."

"Was it a cat I saw."

"I'm, alas, a salami."

There are more palindromes out there! Brainstorm with your friends and see how many you can come up with—it's the perfect thing to do on Topsy Turvy Day!

# Paper and Pencil Games

These games require a little bit more than just your brain—but you can handle it! Grab some paper and pencils, and you're ready to roll!

## Sentence Machine

The scientist works fiendishly with his paper and pencil to get the words just right—then he feeds it into the sentence machine…and out pops a sentence!

**What You'll Need:** Paper, pencil
**Players:** 2 or more

**The first person to be the "scientist" writes a list of five words. The words are totally up to the scientist—anything goes!** Then he slowly reads it to the second player, who is the "sentence machine". The second player has to come up with a sentence using all the scientist's words. But no paper for the sentence machine! He has to try and remember all the words the scientist "fed" him. He gets 1 point for each word he uses in his sentence. For example, if the scientist read the words *feet, piano, chicken, dust,* and *goldfish,* the sentence machine might spit out *"Fred loved to play the piano with his feet while eating chicken, dusting the house, and singing sweetly to his goldfish."* The sentence machine would earn all 5 points for that one! But if the sentence machine didn't remember all the words and said something like, *"The chicken loved to dust the goldfish,"* he'd get 3 points for using three of the words. Take turns being the scientist and the machine, and get ready to hear some pretty wacky sentences!

# CROSSED WORDS

Link words with your friend in your personal crossword puzzle!

**What You'll Need:** Graph paper (or regular paper and a ruler), pencil

**Players:** 2

Mark off a square that contains 15 boxes down and 15 across. Graph paper works best, but if you don't have any, you can use a ruler (or straight edge) to draw the lines on a plain piece of paper. Choose a theme for your puzzle like *"silly names," "TV characters," "people we know,"* or *"things to put on a hamburger"*—anything you want to brainstorm about. The first player thinks of a word that fits in the category and writes it in the center of the puzzle. (One letter to a square!) Now take turns building words and writing them in the boxes. Here's the tricky part: every word has to share a letter with a word that's already on the page. Score 1 point for every letter you use. Once you fill up the grid, or both of you can't think of any more words, add up your points. The player with the most points wins.

## Things to Put On a Hamburger

|   |   |   |   |   | M | U | S | H | R | O | O | M | S |
|---|---|---|---|---|---|---|---|---|---|---|---|---|---|
|   |   |   |   |   |   |   |   |   |   |   |   | U |   |
|   |   |   |   |   | P | E | P | P | E | R | S |   |   |
|   |   |   |   |   | I |   |   |   |   |   | T |   |   |
|   |   |   | L | E | T | T | U | C | E |   |   | A |   |
|   |   |   |   |   |   |   |   | K |   |   |   | R |   |
|   |   | B |   | T |   |   |   | L |   |   | K |   | D |
|   | M | A | Y | O |   | C | H | E | E | S | E |   |   |
|   |   | C |   | M |   | H |   | S |   |   | T |   |   |
|   |   | O |   | A |   | I |   |   |   |   | C |   |   |
|   |   | N |   | T |   | L |   |   |   |   | H |   |   |
|   |   |   |   | O | N | I | O | N |   |   | U |   |   |
|   |   |   |   |   |   |   |   |   |   |   | P |   |   |
|   |   |   |   |   |   |   |   |   |   |   |   |   |   |
|   |   |   |   |   |   |   |   |   |   |   |   |   |   |

### CHALLENGE
Use the whole paper for your grid and make a gigantic puzzle!

74

## FILL IN THE BLANKS

See who can fill in the blanks and make the longest words with this word game!

**What You'll Need:** Paper, pencils (one for each player)
**Players:** 2 or more

Everyone should make three vertical columns on their piece of paper. Pick a word that's four letters or longer and write it down in the left column. Leave the center column blank and write the same word *backward* down the right column. Now all you have to do is fill in the blanks! Add letters to the middle column to make a word using the letters in the left and right columns. For example, if the word you chose was *"cheese,"* your paper could look something like this:

Give yourself 1 point for each letter you use to fill in the blanks. Try and come up with nice, long words and you'll rack up loads of points! The player with the most points at the end wins.

## ALPHABET STORM

**What You'll Need:** Paper, pencils (one for each player)
**Players:** 2 or more

Write the letters of the alphabet down the left side of your paper before you start. You and your friends should think of a topic that you're going to brainstorm, like *"things that would be gross to eat"* or *"things you wouldn't want to swim in"*. Set a time limit and start storming! You'll have to try and think of one word for each letter of the alphabet. For example, if you were doing the topic *"things that would be gross to eat,"* you could put *"ants"* for A, *"bugs"* for B, and C could be *"chalk."* Then you'd keep going until you got through the whole alphabet.

## Survival Tip

You don't have to go in order when you play Alphabet Storm, so if you get stuck on a letter, move on. And if you get an idea for the letter Z before even looking at A, write it down!

When you go over your lists, see how many people came up with the same words. If you want to keep score, you can give 1 point to *only the words that no one else had*. So, for example, if more than one person wrote down *"ant,"* then everyone would cross it off their lists and no one would get the point for it. But if no one else had *"bugs,"* then you'd get the point. So try and think outside the box to rack up the points! The player with the most points, after you compare your lists, wins.

## BALONEY

Make up definitions to crazy words you don't know and see if you can detect the true definition in all the baloney!

**What You'll Need:** A dictionary, paper, pencils (one for each player)
**Players:** 4 or more

Give each player some paper and a pencil. The first player looks through the dictionary for a word that he thinks no one will know. Once he picks his word, he reads it aloud and writes the real definition on a piece of paper. Now, everyone else has baloney on the brain! **Each person invents a definition for the word and writes it down.** Remember, you're trying to get people to choose your definition, so try to be convincing! What does the word sound like it could mean? Do you think it's an action? Or does it sound more like an object? Maybe it's a rare disease or fungus? Baloney it up!

After you've written your fake definition, fold it up and pass it to the player who picked the word. Once he has a definition from every player, he reads each one aloud (including the real definition). Now everyone tries to guess (except for the person who picked the word) which is the correct one (don't vote for your own fake definition!). **If you guess right, you get a point. You also get a point if someone else chooses your made-up definition as the correct one.** For example, if the word chosen is *"nib,"* which definition would you think was correct? Does *nib* mean: *"the pad on the bottom of an animal's foot," "the point of a pen,"* or *"the act of stealing someone's napkin"*? If you guessed *"the point of a pen,"* then you'd get a point! If you guessed either of the other definitions, the player who wrote the definition would get the point! Take turns picking words out of the dictionary, and whoever has the most points, when you call it quits, wins.

# A Field Day for Your Brain
## Magazine Scavenger Hunt

So you and your friend are hanging around the house, wondering what to do. If you have a bunch of old magazines or catalogs sitting around, look no further!

**What You'll Need:** Paper, pencils, some old magazines (at least one for each player), scissors (one for each player)
**Players:** 2 or more

Just like in a real scavenger hunt, you first need to **make a list of the things you and your friend want to search for**. This is half the fun—you guys can make the list up to be whatever you want, so get creative! Will your list have a theme (like smelly stuff or things you'd find under you bed), or is it totally random (like a pumpkin and an old sneaker)? Will it include specific words or just pictures? What kinds of pictures will you search for? A pair of sunglasses? A big toe? How about a mustache? Once your list is done, have each player make a copy, and then start searching! When you find an item, cut it out and set it aside. Once a player is done looking through a magazine, he should throw it into the middle, so someone else can take a look. See who finds all the items on the list first—that player is the winner!

## Survival Tip

To keep track of everything, it's a good idea to check off your list as you go. You don't want to waste time finding doubles!

### SNEAKY TIP

Speed is important to winning, so remember to be creative while searching. If "hand" is on the list—any hand will do. For example, you could find a human hand, an alien hand, or even a hand on a clock. Any of these would count, so keep an open mind!

**IDEA:** If you have a few friends over, divide up into two competing teams and see which team is full of faster scavengers!

# IT'S NOT JUNK, IT'S ART!

*"One man's junk is another man's treasure,"* is what they say. So why not find some junk and see if you can spin it into gold?

**What You'll Need:** Any old "junk" you can find, cardboard, glue, paint and brushes (optional), your imagination
**Players:** 1 or more

If you're ready to become a junk artist, the first thing you need is some junk! Start by collecting things. **Look around. Are there things in the house that no one wants anymore? Stuff they might donate to your art?** Go in your basement, garage, or anywhere else that things accumulate, and see what you can find (make sure you get permission first). Take anything that you think might be able to help with your creations. Collect interesting boxes, egg cartons, bottle caps, cardboard tubes, gift wrap, buttons, paper clips, Styrofoam trays, straws—you get the idea. Let your imagination run wild!

Once you have enough stuff, go create! It's a good idea to start with a flat piece of cardboard as your base and sculpt your objects on top. When you have a piece where you want it, glue it into place. After the glue dries, you can paint your sculpture, or leave it as it is for a natural look.

## It's Not Junk, It's My Invention!

Do you ever wonder what it would be like to be a scientist in a laboratory inventing things? Have you ever wished that someone would invent something you have in mind? Like an automatic pizza feeder, or sneakers with headlights? Don't wait—use some of that junk you've collected to invent on your own! When you're collecting things for your junk art, does anything spark an idea for an invention? Get together with a friend and see what you can come up with!

# Boredom Busters Forever!

**W**ay to go! You made it to the end of this book and that means you're smart enough to know that *knowledge is power*. **By learning some new games and fun things to do, you're now fully armed and prepared to tackle any tricks Boredom might throw your way.** (Maybe Boredom should start looking for a new hobby!)

Hopefully, you've not only had a blast playing these games, but you've come to realize that, with imagination, you can find fun in any situation. How can Boredom compete with that?

And just think—now that you've survived all those times when (you *used* to think) you had nothing to do, you can handle anything!